ALSO BY CARL I. GABLE

Murano Magic (2004)

recitalist played the first half of the program on the 1732 organ, perched high over the north choir stalls, creating a simple, sweet singing tone. For the second half of the program he crossed to the 1794 organ, whose flute and reed stops produced a much more complex and colorful—though no more beautiful—sound.

Carl leads Giacomo and Silvana into the Frari's Cornaro Piscopia Chapel, added at the north end of the main altar in about 1420 by Giovanni Cornaro of the family's Piscopia branch. Although ostensibly created to honor Saint Mark, the patron saint of Venice, the chapel has as its highlight a statuary monument depicting an angel with a scroll eulogizing the patron's father. One writer calls it "one of the most beautiful monuments of the Venetian Renaissance." Nonetheless, many guidebooks mention it only in passing, if at all.

Next we shuttle the Miolos to the sacristy on the opposite side of the church. The wall facing the entrance features an elaborate marble installation deeply carved in dramatic late-baroque figures by Francesco Cabianca, whose brother Bortolo in 1716 created the putti and other stucco decorations at our own Villa Cornaro. For Giacomo, however, the highlight of the Frari—his favorite sight of the whole day—is the *Madonna and Child* of Giovanni Bellini above the altar of the refectory. The enthroned Madonna is serene, mysterious, oblivious to the cherub musicians playing at her feet.

"*Una meraviglia, una meraviglia.* A miracle," Giacomo murmurs over and over.

On our way toward the Rialto Bridge we stop for an espresso and brioche. I watch with amusement as Giacomo discreetly studies the small *caffè*, evaluating it with the trained eye of a competitor. He solemnly agrees with us that Caffè Palladio is handsomer—and has better prices to boot.

We proceed like chickens: three steps forward, then a pause. Giacomo finds a constant stream of new things to stop and inspect: a Gothic building facade, a strangely shaped chimney, an old religious plaque mounted high on a wall. At the church of San Salvatore we point out the tomb of Queen Caterina Cornaro and her

funeral monument carved by Bernardino Contino in the early
1580s—less than ten years before our own statue of her at Villa
Cornaro was created by Camillo Mariani.

From San Salvatore we detour to show Giacomo and Silvana the
lugubrious face carved at the base of the campanile of the church of
Santa Maria Formosa. With his usual hyperbole, Ruskin describes
it as "huge, inhuman, and monstrous,—leering in bestial degrada-
tion, too foul to be either pictured or described, or to be beheld for
more than an instant." Giacomo laughs at its grotesqueness, and
we all wonder what inspired such a decoration.

We finish the tour with visits to the church of Santi Giovanni e
Paolo to see the grave and funeral monument of Doge Marco
Cornaro, and to the church of the Holy Apostles, where Giorgio
Cornaro—the brother of Queen Caterina Cornaro—is buried in a
richly detailed chapel in which both Mauro Codussi and Tullio
Lombardo had a hand.

By this time we are all dragging a bit, and Carl and I are con-
cerned that we have worn out our tourists by trying to see too
much. We have a late lunch at a small hotel near the train station—
a meal distinguished more by the company than the food—and
rest our legs on the train ride back to Piombino Dese.

The next morning, when Silvana arrives to open the shutters at
the villa, she brings along a street map of Venice. Will we please
trace our itinerary on it? she asks. She and Giacomo want to keep it
as a reminder of the day. Carl and I retain our own memories of the
day as well; we felt that we were a part of the fabric of the city, like
natives showing our home.

A pleasant group of about twenty visitors from Houston has just
finished its tour through the ground floor of the villa. On the south
portico I've explained and translated the graffiti and sent them off
into the park, recommending that they walk to the seven-arch
bridge for the view back at the villa's south facade. I also ask that
they exit the grounds by walking around the side of the villa to the
front gate, instead of tracking grass clippings and morning dew

back through the grand salon. One woman tarries to speak with me.

"How fortunate that you and your husband are both passionate about the same thing!" she says.

Her remark startles me. I have never considered the possibility that Carl might have fallen in love with the villa but not I. Or that I might have been enamored by these bricks and *intonaco,* but Carl not.

Yet it could have happened that way. How fortuitous, how unlikely, that we both find in our villa, in Venice, in Italy a source of such infinite fascination.

Villa Cornaro has been the cornerstone of it all. Like a great athletic coach, the villa is at once a disciplinarian, a trainer, and a motivator.

You can step onto new stages and play new roles, the villa whispers. Find your hidden pools of strength, open yourself to see art with fresh and wider-ranging eyes, examine whole new palettes of color in your everyday life, vault past barriers of language, culture, and habit.

All to better care for me, my villa tells me.

53

Groundhog Day

Often in Italy I feel like Bill Murray in the film *Groundhog Day.* The same day is repeated over and over. Each evening I sit on the south portico, mesmerized by the swallows in their timeless gyres. I watch the Cagnins at work in their field across the bridge, or hear their tractor's struggling chug when they pass out of sight. Ilario Mariotto and his brother Silvano work their own fields to the west. Sometimes the crop is corn, sometimes oats or barley; sometimes the field lies fallow for a season. But the same cycle is forever repeated, summer and winter. This portico where I'm sitting has overlooked these fields for 450 years. The Cagnins' complaining tractor has replaced a team of oxen that were probably equally plaintive; the Cagnins own the field instead of sharecropping for the Cornaros, but the pattern of everyday life is unchanging.

The national scene gives me the same impression as I puzzle my way through the newspaper account of each day's meaningless changes. The fall of governments follows the fall of governments, bribery scandals succeed bribery scandals, soaring budget deficits surpass soaring budget deficits, *scioperi* (labor strikes) follow more *scioperi.*

Rome is the Eternal City, I think to myself, not because it's ancient but because absolutely nothing ever really changes.

But then I am awakened by a remark from Silvana at a dinner party for some friends—the Miolos, the Battistons, the Bighins, the Cechettos. Silvana is speaking to Lino Cechetto, but I overhear her.

"The Mariottos are the last real *contadini*," she says, using a word that once denoted peasant farmers and now applies to landowning small-scale farmers as well. Silvana is actually focusing on that peasant tradition. "Ilario farms in all the old ways, uses no fertilizers or insect sprays, shares his home with his cows, makes his own wine from the grapes that he grows, has his own fruit and vegetable garden behind his house," she continues.

Silvana leaves me wondering if my original perception has been essentially flawed. These traditions that I see every day, repeating the daily life of centuries, may be in their last generation. Then the *contadini*—and the way of life they epitomize—will disappear.

The same may be true on the national level. While nothing seems changed on a daily basis, the contrasts in Italy's political life over time are startling. Rome's government-by-splinter-party has lurched suddenly toward a two-party system. At least the parties have begun to organize themselves into alliances of the center-left and center-right for major elections.

I'm led to ponder Villa Cornaro itself. Is it the solid and immutable rock that I have always envisioned? Or will it, too, be changed by the transformations that surround it?

When I first came to Piombino Dese, bicycles filled the racks at the Battistons' *supermercato*. Women would purchase only as many groceries as they could carry in two or three plastic bags on their handlebars; they bicycled home through the Via Roma gauntlet of trucks and autos. Now cars crowd the recently expanded parking lot. Women are still the predominant shoppers, but most drive their own cars.

Many more women work outside the home today than when I first arrived. They drive to dozens of small *fabbriche* dotting the outskirts of Piombino Dese, or they drive to work at shops in nearby towns. Last Saturday evening Nazzareno joked—but with nostalgia—about Italian women turning into American women, driving their own cars, spending their own money, tending less to homemaking and cooking. *Nidi*—literally "nests," but signifying child-care centers—have sprung up in town, both church-sponsored and private, to care for the small children of working mothers. Some working mothers rely on a network of babysitters and their own mothers, but often the grandmothers are working themselves and other would-be babysitters want full-time employment with better wages and pension benefits.

A take-out pizza parlor appeared last year on Via della Vittoria; it even delivers if you telephone your order. Efficiency is breaking out in state-owned enterprises: staffing in the Piombino Dese train station has shrunk from three workers per shift to just one, as preprinted tickets have replaced the handwritten ones that prevailed earlier.

Creeping multinationalism invades the school curriculum. English, once a specialized elective, is taught in elementary school in Piombino Dese, with children as young as six receiving three hours of instruction a week. When we first arrived in Piombino Dese I had to speak Italian in order to communicate even the simplest observation or need; abstruse terms—*rubinetto* (faucet), *scaldabagno* (water heater), *fognatura* (sewage), and *fossa* (ditch)—salted my new vocabulary. Now many young people speak English well, including Riccardo Miolo and Elisa, Leonardo's *fidanzata*.

We can debate whether take-out pizza and English fluency are positive developments or negative, but some of the changes taking place are undeniably for the worse. Michela Scquizzato tells me that her *telefonino* (cell phone) was lifted while she was shopping at Battiston's. For the last several years, upon leaving the autostrada at the Padova Ovest exit near Limena, we have come to expect a clutch of prostitutes standing beside the road, not just at night but throughout the afternoon. Pulling out from the parking lot of Barbesin, a favorite restaurant near Castelfranco, we are puzzled by the erratic driving of the car ahead of us. Finally we realize that the driver is slowing to inspect the prostitutes strung like gaudy beads along the roadside. Albanians, the newspaper accounts say. The warfare and unrest in the Balkans since the fall of Communism bring boatloads of illegal immigrants across the narrow Adriatic Sea every night. Once in Italy, the immigrants must find an employer willing to hire them without work permits or else drift into burglary, prostitution, or other crime. Albanian gangs are said to be providing competition for the Italian *mafiosi*. Our Italian friends are as shocked as we to learn one May morning that two young Piombino Dese boys have discovered the body of a murdered Albanian prostitute in the industrial district of town; we find only minimum comfort in the police theory that the body was merely dumped in Piombino Dese after the murder occurred elsewhere. In the same month, burglars attempt to explode their way into the ATM machine at the branch of Banca Ambrosiana just down Via Roma, and nighttime vandals try to burn the mammoth wooden doors of the parish church by setting fire to oil-soaked rags they have tacked onto them.

Italy seems certain to survive it all. In his last year in office, Prime Minister Giuliano Amato exhorted his countrymen to respect the tax laws. "Of course we expect a businessman to buy a fur coat for his mistress," he said understandingly, "but he should not deduct it on his taxes as a business expense."

When Silvio Berlusconi, Amato's successor, complained about having to move into Palazzo Chigi, the official government residence, because "the food is horrible," Italians *understood*. Good food binds Italians in a way that will, I'm sure, survive government efficiency, English fluency, and the euro, just as market day will survive e-commerce.

And Villa Cornaro? Is it fated to change, to modernize and homogenize? I want to avoid being a Pollyanna; the ability of an ancient structure to survive in the modern world cannot be assumed. One thing I have learned: Villa Cornaro is a part of its community. Villa Cornaro will prosper as long as it retains the respect, love, and protection of its people. The modern world needs Villa Cornaro as a token of a civilized past and as a vibrant part of the present; posterity can take the preservation of it in our time as a token of our own civilization.

Coda

We are in Piombino Dese on September 11, 2001. Italian television starts following the horrific events in New York and Washington, D.C., within minutes of their onset, so we are apprised of developments as they unfold. Sympathetic phone calls from local friends begin immediately, offering condolences and *solidarietà*. Francesca arrives at the gate to give me a hug; Bianca embraces me when I enter the *supermercato*. Silvana weeps when she arrives in the evening to close the *balcone*, expressing her bewilderment at the madmen of the world. One friend appears at the front gate the next day with a plate of food, as though we have had a death in the family and need something to comfort us.

Hurrying along Via Roma the following week, I am hailed from behind by the elderly local pharmacist. His daughter usually staffs the counter in his shop, and he and I have never shared more than a *buon giorno*. He expresses in traditional terms his sorrow at the recent tragedy, but asks me to wait until he shows me something.

"*Un attimo, un attimo, signora.* One moment," he says as he pulls out his wallet and searches through it. He finds the item he is seeking and holds it out for me to take: a recent newspaper clipping. I unfold it to discover an Italian translation of "God Bless America." He waits for me to read the verses, then retrieves the clipping, refolds it, and returns it to his wallet.

I stand and watch as he walks away and disappears among my neighbors.

Appendix 1

Si Mangia Bene in Italia

Living in Italy inspires even the most creativity-deficient gene to mutate. Long ago I accepted that I must be an energetic admirer of creative endeavor because of the absence of any personal aptitude for it.

But Italy! Italy has taught me to reconsider. Italy celebrates daily every cook's good food, every woman's flower display, every woman's bold scarf arrangement. Every community promotes art shows for local artists, exhibitions for workers in decorative iron. To encourage its lamp industry, Piombino Dese sponsors a local competition in lamp design. Italy *expects* artistic enterprise from everyone.

So I join in where I can, drawn to experimentation in the kitchen, artful presentation of food in the dining room. But first, I copy: my Italian diaries are laced with local recipes and notes on Venetan food and the way the Venetans serve it. The recipes are simple, the dishes are presented with great fantasy, and the food is delicious.

I tease Francesca and Wilma, telling them I want to prepare a cookbook of their recipes and will follow them around for a week, Naomi-like, to jot down the recipe for every dish they prepare. They laugh and say such a book will never sell; their food is too simple. I think the simplicity is what makes it special.

Here are two simple vegetable recipes from Wilma.

WILMA'S EASY PEPERONI

2 sweet red peppers
2 yellow peppers
2 tablespoons olive oil
1 clove garlic, crushed
Salt and pepper

Cut up the red peppers and yellow peppers into large squares, being sure to remove any membrane. Place in a frying pan with the olive oil. Cover and cook over high heat until the peppers are sizzling, then reduce the heat and simmer, covered, for 20 to 25 minutes until they are softened but still firm. Turn off the heat and let sit for 20 minutes.

Transfer the peppers and oil to a small bowl. Add the crushed garlic, and salt and pepper to taste. Cover with plastic wrap. Let sit several hours before serving.

A variation is to include several anchovy fillets with the peppers.

WILMA'S PLUM TOMATOES

8 to 12 fresh plum tomatoes
½ cup dry white wine
Bread crumbs
Salt and pepper
Fresh basil, chopped
Olive oil

Preheat the oven to 375°F. Cut the plum tomatoes in half lengthwise. Arrange the halves in a baking pan, cut side up. Pour the white wine around them. Lightly cover each tomato half with bread crumbs; then drizzle with olive oil. Sprinkle with salt and pepper and chopped fresh basil. Bake for 25 minutes. (This can be prepared early in the day; just reheat under a low-heat broiler for 5 to 8 minutes before serving.)

Serve as a first course with *burrata* mozzarella and thinly sliced firm bread.

Every woman in the Veneto prides herself on her culinary skills. Carl and I regularly begin our sojourns in Piombino Dese with several small dinner parties, inviting six or eight friends each evening. Our object is to greet friends, learn local gossip, and awaken our hibernating Italian tongues. The evenings also produce something much more valuable than mere news. They spur a food contest to rival *The Iron Chef*. Each wife invites us to dinner in the ensuing three or four weeks, plotting her meal as she would a military campaign.

Last night, for example, Silvana—who opens Caffè Palladio every morning at five and spends her Monday "day off" cleaning the premises—reciprocated our dinner of three weeks ago with a banquet for twelve. Her first sortie consisted of prosecco with antipasti: small soft balls of white mozzarella, sweet chunks of orange cantaloupe, tangy strips of red-brown sun-dried tomatoes, smooth black Sicilian olives. This course was served on their patio; Giacomo's forty rosebushes and thirty caged songbirds provided the backdrop. On Silvana's request, we moved inside to their long, narrow table for the *primo piatto*, served in two handsome tureens:

SILVANA'S PEA SOUP

2 pounds fresh peas
1 quart chicken broth
1 small yellow onion, chopped
Parsley
2 cups béchamel
½ cup grated Parmesan cheese

Shell the peas. Simmer them for 1 hour with ½ cup of the broth, the chopped onion, and several sprigs of parsley. Puree, then add to the rest of the broth. Heat to a simmer.

Prepare separately a béchamel made with 4 tablespoons butter, 3 tablespoons flour, 2 cups milk. Blend it into the broth, along with the grated Parmesan, stirring constantly. When the soup is blended and hot, serve with a good crusty bread.

Next at Silvana's party came whisper-thin slices of roast beef accompanied by a colorful palette of fresh vegetables, simmered *en brodo*, and a salad with as many colors as Joseph's coat.

A truncheon of cheeses—Parmesan, *mezzano*, *Montasio*—followed, then large bowls of chilled, almost black cherries and plump green grapes. Then fruit tortes, followed by *fior di latte* (a flavor similar to vanilla) *gelato* crowned with fresh sweet strawberries that had been soaked in *limoncello* liqueur. Giacomo was the wine sergeant throughout, refilling glasses and then consummating the campaign with liqueurs of dizzying variety. Conversation flowed as rapidly and amiably as the wine.

Nazzareno Mason greets our arrival one spring with a large bunch of white asparagus. One stalk is as thick as the handle of our hammer, but Nazzareno assures me this will be the tenderest of all. The asparagus was pulled from his cousin's garden just thirty minutes earlier. He tells me how to cook it:

NAZZARENO'S WHITE ASPARAGUS

First, buy only asparagus with a credible claim to being very fresh. Peel each stalk, not with a knife (which would remove too much pulp) but with a vegetable peeler. Tie the bundle securely with string and place it upright in a narrow but deep pot, with water covering only the bottom two inches of the stalks. (Best: buy an asparagus steamer, which holds the stalks upright off the pan bottom.) Steam for 20 to 40 minutes, depending on the size of the stalks and their age. Test the stalks with a knife. When they are tender but not mushy, pull them from the water.

Memi Scquizzato taught us how to eat white asparagus our first spring in Piombino Dese. You place several tender stalks on your plate beside two halves of hard-boiled egg. Dress with a drizzle of deep green olive oil, a drop or two of balsamic vinegar, and lots of salt and pepper. Mash the eggs finely with a fork, then munch with bites of asparagus.

Surely the Olympian gods dined on this vegetable regularly!

Ham, glorious ham! One of our favorite treats in Italy is prosciutto— preferably the San Daniele variety. I learned several years ago from an Acquarello tape that there are three kinds of prosciutto, each from a different area of northern Italy and each with a somewhat different curing process. Parma prosciutto is known for its tangy bite, its piquancy; San Daniele prosciutto is sweeter—and is my favorite accompaniment for chilled melon slices or luscious split figs. The third type, Veneto prosciutto, combines the intense savoriness of Parma and the sweetness of San Daniele, but much less of it is produced. In the production process, the raw hams are packed in sea salt for a week, then exposed to mountain air for a twelve-to-twenty-month curing period. No wonder prosciutto is so expensive!

In May the Veneto imports from Sicily pale green melons the size of large softballs. The melons have luscious red-orange flesh and we devour one every day until Battiston's supply runs out. We often combine them with bright slices of San Daniele prosciutto. Cristiano, a regular behind the Battistons' meat counter, always prepares a perfect bed of slices, lean but with fat enough for flavor, thin but not torn.

In September we eat the prosciutto with our own fat purple figs from the two trees on either side of our south portico. I like the figs peeled and halved, set atop the bed of prosciutto like "Sweet Nothings" miniature roses. Fresh, thinly sliced white pears are another good accompaniment for prosciutto and can be assembled into a flower design for the prosciutto platter.

I have not passed a single day in Italy without learning of a new type of food, a new way of cooking food, or a new way to enjoy food. Last week, at a dinner at the Zambons'—they live across the street and have unquestionably the finest view of the villa from their balcony—Lucianna placed on the table a large wheel of a platter bearing a brilliant garden of baked stuffed vegetables. Her mother's recipe, she said. It was both beautiful and delicious.

LUCIANNA'S STUFFED VEGETABLES

5 sweet peppers (medium-size, not huge)
4 ripe round tomatoes
4 long eggplants
4 zucchini
1 pound lean beef and 1 pound lean pork, ground together twice
Parsley, chopped fine
1 clove garlic, chopped fine
2 eggs, beaten
3/4 cup grated Parmesan cheese
1 1/2 cups milk
3 slices American-type commercial bread, cut in cubes, then soaked
    in the milk (above)
Salt and pepper
Ground nutmeg
Vegetable oil (not olive oil)
Bouillon powder

Preheat the oven to 300°F.

Wash and core the peppers and tomatoes, leaving the bottoms unpierced. Cut the eggplants and the zucchini in half; remove the pulp from each piece with a teaspoon. Set aside.

To make the stuffing, combine the ground meat, parsley, garlic, eggs, Parmesan, milk-soaked bread cubes, salt and pepper, and a pinch of nutmeg. Mix well.

Stuff the vegetables loosely with the meat mixture. Drizzle them with oil and dust lightly with bouillon powder.

Bake for $1\frac{1}{2}$ to 2 hours, turning regularly. The vegetables are done when the shells are soft but not mushy. Halve or quarter the vegetables, then arrange them attractively on a large platter.

When I prepared this recipe for the first time, I discussed with Stefano, the butcher, what I was making and the need for him to grind the meats together. A woman waiting at the door shot up to the counter and said, "Oh yes, this is one of my own recipes! You must grind the meat together twice and then be sure that you don't pack the vegetables too firmly."

That afternoon this same woman was bicycling south on Via Roma in front of the villa and pulled to a stop when she saw me standing on the curb to cross the street.

"*Ah, signora,*" she said. "You will make delicious vegetables if you just follow my advice. I am known throughout the town as an excellent cook!" And she sped off.

My favorite of all Venetan meats is veal served with a tuna sauce. It may sound difficult, but it's not. The recipe, however, has one challenge: the veal must be sliced very, very thin so that it absorbs the tuna flavor; this requires slicing it when it is cold, preferably using a commercial meat slicer, which most of my Italian friends count among their kitchen appliances.

The butcher at the Battistons' *supermercato* provides me with a lean four-pound veal roast, more than enough for our party for twelve tomorrow. He's tied it securely, and I've bought a special oblong cooking pot that the roast barely fits into so that it won't swim in liquid. Now I'm ready to try Gabriella's recipe.

GABRIELLA'S VITELLO TONNATO

1 carrot
1 celery stalk
1 onion
1 vegetable bouillon cube
1 lean veal roast (3 to 4 pounds)
10 anchovy fillets
$\frac{1}{3}$ cup fresh lemon juice
$\frac{1}{3}$ cup small capers
2 6-ounce cans tuna (preferably Italian) in oil
$1\frac{1}{2}$ cups olive oil
2 cups Hellmann's mayonnaise

Bring to a boil in a large, heavy pot about 1½ quarts of water with the carrot, celery stalk, onion, and boullion cube. Add the roast, taking care that the water comes up to the top of the roast (if not, add boiling water). Bring back to a boil and simmer gently for several hours, until the veal is tender to the prick of a knife. (I simmered my 4-pound roast for 2½ hours.)

Take the pot off the heat and let cool for at least four hours before removing the roast from the liquid. Then chill the roast for several hours or overnight, for easier slicing.

The tuna sauce is quick and easy. Blend well in the food processor: the anchovy fillets, lemon juice, capers, tuna fish, and olive oil. When the mixture is smooth, add the mayonnaise (Gabriella makes her own mayonnaise, but I carry Hellmann's from Atlanta) and blend in well.

Slice the veal as thin as possible without shredding the meat. (I use my bread-slicing knife.) Spread some tuna sauce on the bottom of a long, deep dish or platter, then arrange slices of veal on top; repeat until the veal and sauce are all layered, ending with a sauce layer. Cover tightly with plastic wrap (after placing toothpicks at even intervals across the meat in order to keep the plastic away from the surface) and refrigerate at least overnight.

Serve within the next week.

I love this dish, so I always hope there are leftovers from a party!

Carl's favorite vegetables are those I roast in the oven, following a recipe given me years ago by an Italian-American friend of our daughter Ashley. *Molto semplice!*

CHRISTINA'S ROAST VEGETABLES

3 potatoes
3 zucchini
2 large sweet peppers, red or yellow
3 onions
1 fennel bulb
⅓ cup extra-virgin olive oil
Salt and pepper

Preheat the oven to 400°F. Wash and peel the potatoes and cut them crosswise into ½-inch slices. Scrub the zucchini and slice them lengthwise in quarters, then halve these. Cut the peppers into 1-inch strips, then halve the strips. Quarter the onions. Remove the top and base from the fennel bulb, then cut the bulb vertically to make slices about ½ inch thick. Place all the vegetables on a towel for five to ten minutes to remove excess water.

Place the vegetables in a large bowl and dribble with the olive oil, mixing thoroughly to coat. Spread the vegetables evenly on a single large, shallow baking pan or two smaller ones; don't let your pieces overlap. Season with salt and pepper.

Pop the pan into the oven and bake for 25 to 30 minutes, turning every 8 to 10 minutes. If the vegetables brown too quickly, turn down the heat.

Supper at Wilma and Paolo's apartment is, as always, a feast for the eyes as well as for the stomach, as the pastor's wife said to Anne in one of my favorite passages from *Anne of Green Gables*. White plates on a pale blue cloth. Yellow chrysanthemums on pale blue paper napkins. Medium-blue glasses to hold our Gavi wine. The first course is so simple the recipe might seem hardly worth jotting down. But several times it has saved me when we have unexpected guests on a Wednesday afternoon and all the stores including the Battistons' are *chiusi*—closed.

WILMA'S SIMPLE TOMATO SAUCE

1 yellow onion, chopped
Olive oil
4 or 5 fresh tomatoes (or 1 can good plum tomatoes), chopped
Salt and pepper
Pasta
Smoked cheese, such as ricotta *affumicata*

Sauté the chopped onion in olive oil until soft. Add the chopped fresh tomatoes and simmer for 20 minutes. (If using canned tomatoes, drain them and chop them, then simmer for 10 minutes.) Blend lightly in a food processor. Season with salt and pepper to taste.

Serve on a bed of interesting pasta such as *orecchiette* (little ears) or *farfalle* (butterflies) cooked al dente. Top with the grated smoked cheese.

Last Sunday Francesca introduced me to her fried zucchini blossoms.

FRANCESCA'S DELICATE FRY

8 fresh zucchini blossoms
24 fresh sage leaves
1 egg
$\frac{1}{4}$ cup beer (preferably flat)
$\frac{1}{4}$ cup flour
$\frac{1}{2}$ teaspoon salt
Peanut oil

Rinse the zucchini blossoms. Cut each blossom along one side and spread it out flat on a paper towel to dry. Rinse the sage leaves and dry them on paper towels.

Beat the egg with $\frac{1}{4}$ cup water, the beer, the flour, and the salt.

Heat oil over medium-high heat. Dip the zucchini blossoms and sage leaves in the batter, then fry in hot—not smoking—peanut oil (about $\frac{1}{2}$ inch deep) for two to three minutes, turning once. Dry on paper towels and serve as an antipasto, with crackers and a soft cheese such as Robiolo.

As I draw these favorite recipes from several years of notes, it seems that I am eating at Francesca's or Wilma's every evening. Although I try to reciprocate with equal taste and fantasy, my efforts seldom reach their standards. But I keep trying and, right now, *tocca a me.* It's my turn.

Appendix 2

A Sixty-Second Guide to Venice

All of Venice is a museum! You only need to wander the streets, without going in anywhere, to experience some of the world's great Gothic and Renaissance treasures. And if you choose to step into some church that you are passing—almost any church—you'll stumble upon some painting or sculpture by a famous Renaissance artist. In other words, you don't really need a guidebook to tell you where to go.

Buy a guidebook anyway! (It will tell you where you are when you get there.) And, of course, a street map. (The ones in the guidebooks are helpful, but frequently not detailed enough.) Here are our favorites:

- Sheila Hale, *The American Express Pocket Travel Guide: Venice.*
- Hugh Honour, *The Companion Guide to Venice.*

SOME KEY SIGHTS

1. *Piazza di San Marco.* There's a good reason why St. Mark's Plaza is the most touristy, crowded place in Venice: It's filled with incredible monuments!

Basilica di San Marco. Is it "a treasure heap . . . hollowed beneath five great vaulted porches" (Ruskin) or "like a vast and warty bug taking a meditative walk" (Twain)? Be sure to go inside. Don't miss the Pala d'Oro-golden altar screen—and the museum up the stairs near the front entrance. Small admissions for each.

Doge's Palace. An architectural masterpiece steeped in the history of Venice, which was an independent and powerful empire for more than a thousand years, ending with the surrender to Napoléon in 1797. Everything is here: council rooms, art treasures, dungeons. Allocate an hour minimum.

Campanile (Bell Tower) and the Loggetta at its base. Wonderful view of Venice from the top of the Campanile, if you have the time.

View (across the basin of the Grand Canal). That's Palladio's spectacular church of San Giorgio Maggiore sitting on the island across the way.

Everything else in sight.

2. *Rialto Bridge.* Hustling, bustling shops, souvenirs, view of the Grand Canal in two directions. Prices here are generally better than at Piazza di San Marco.

3. *Grand Canal,* via vaporetto or gondola. The No. 1 vaporetto (boat bus) gives a slow and majestic (sometimes crowded and hot) ride along the whole length of the Grand Canal, allowing you to view all the palaces from the water, which is their principal facade. (Many vaporetti go two ways; be sure you get the one going in the direction you want!) Or for an infinitely more romantic (and pricey) view of the Grand Canal and other, smaller canals, spring for an hour (i.e., 45–50 minutes in gondolier time) on a gondola one evening near sunset.

4. *Accademia.* Venice's major museum for paintings. The number of visitors allowed inside at one time is restricted; this policy can result in a long waiting line outside during busy times of day.

5. *Church of San Zaccaria.* A somewhat arbitrary selection from the many incredible churches. The facade shows Gothic styling on the ground level (architect: Gambello) shifting to Renaissance motifs on the floors above (architect: Codussi). Inside, look (left aisle) for Giovanni Bellini's masterwork, *Sacred Conversation.* Don't miss the sacristy and crypt (small admission fee).

6. *Church of the Frari* and *School of San Rocco* (beside each other). The Frari is filled with treasures, including Titian's famous *Assumption of the Virgin* over the central altar. San Rocco's walls are covered with all the Tintoretto paintings you could possibly want to see, plus two or three.

Acknowledgments

The story of our years in Piombino Dese should make clear the support and encouragement we have received from all directions. Nonetheless, we feel a need to acknowledge specially a few individuals for the friendship and tireless assistance they have bestowed on us personally, and the protection and interest they have extended to Villa Cornaro.

Giacomo and Silvana Miolo and their sons, Leonardo and Riccardo, together with Ilario and Giovannina Mariotto, have been the linchpins of our Italian experience, loving and defending Villa Cornaro as fiercely as we do ourselves.

We are grateful to Monsignor Aldo Roma and to Mayor Luciano Cagnin and his predecessors for responding to every call that we have made for their advice and assistance. We have benefited as well from the care and protection that the office of the Superintendent of Fine Arts in Venice extends to Villa Cornaro and all the other great treasures the Veneto shares with the world.

Others who have been critical to our experience include Richard and Julia Rush for entrusting Villa Cornaro to our care, Douglas Lewis for his extraordinary pioneering research that opened our eyes to the fascinating history of our villa and the Cornaro family, and Lola Butler for her tenacity and good humor in teaching us Italian.

Our children love Villa Cornaro as much as we do, and each assisted in bringing this book about. Ashley inspired our efforts with her own writing career and offered valuable comments on an early draft, Carl assisted us in assembling photos, and Jim consistently encouraged us.

Ogden Robertson, Blaine Wiley, and Jean-François Jaussaud have taken beautiful photographs of the villa and generously allowed us to use them here. The enthusiasm and assistance of our editor, Ann Close, and our literary agent, Kitty Benedict, deserve special mention, as does the foresight of Lydia Somerville in bringing us together. Branko Mitrovic graciously reviewed several technical sections of the text for us. We thank them all.

Sally and Carl Gable
May 2005

Photographic Credits

Grateful acknowledgment is made to the following for use of illustrations
appearing on the pages indicated:

Jean-François Jaussaud, pages 11, 133, 228
Wiley-Robertson Photography, pages ii–iii, 77, 78, 129, 213, 226
Local Piombino Dese collections, pages 97, 98

All other illustrations are from the authors' collection.

When they met in the year following their college graduation, Sally and Carl Gable were surprised to learn that they had been undergraduate classmates. They married two years later, following Carl's law school graduation, and now have three children and four grandchildren.

Sally's professional and community activities have centered on music and education. After earning a Master of Music degree, she was music director of an Atlanta church for five years and has continued, as a volunteer, to teach music to preschool children. Sally has served as a trustee of Radcliffe College (now part of Harvard University) and as a member of the board of directors of the Atlanta Symphony Orchestra and the Atlanta Committee for Public Education.

Carl's career has been divided between law practice (corporate and international law) and business (manufacturing). He has served as a director and officer of various nonprofit organizations, including Spoleto Festival USA, the Atlantic Opera, the Carlos Museum of Emory University, and the Center for Palladian Studies in America.

A NOTE ON THE TYPE

The text of this book was set in a typeface called Aldus, designed by the cele-brated typographer Hermann Zapf in 1952–1953. Based on the classical propor-tion of the popular Palatino type family, Aldus was originally adapted for Linotype composition as a slightly lighter version that would read better in smaller sizes.

Hermann Zapf was born in Nuremberg, Germany, in 1918. He has created many other well known typefaces including Comenius, Hunt Roman, Mar-coni, Melior, Michelangelo, Optima, Saphir, Sistina, Zapf Book and Zapf Chancery.

Composed by North Market Street Graphics,
Lancaster, Pennsylvania

Printed and bound by R.R. Donnelley & Sons
Harrisonburg, Virginia

Designed by Soonyoung Kwon